TEXTILES

© Aladdin Books Ltd 1988

Designed and produced by
Aladdin Books Ltd
70 Old Compton Street
London W1V 5PA

First published in
Great Britain in 1988 by
Franklin Watts Ltd
12a Golden Square
London W1R 4BA

ISBN 0 86313 767 9

Printed in Belgium

Author	Kathryn Whyman (Science teacher & author of many children's books)
Design	David West Children's Book Design
Editor	Margaret Fagan
Researcher	Cecilia Weston-Baker
Illustrators	Louise Nevett Simon Bishop
Consultant	Edna Mulligan (Formerly of the Textile Institute)

CONTENTS

Photographic Credits
Cover and page 25: Spectrum; title page and page 23: Tony Stone; pages 4-5 and 9: Photosource; pages 7 and 9: Art Directors; page 13: Courtauld Institute; pages 15 and 17: Hutchison Library; pages 18 and 21: Robert Harding.

TEXTILES

Kathryn Whyman

GLOUCESTER PRESS
London · New York · Toronto · Sydney

WHAT IS A TEXTILE?

A textile was originally a woven fabric. But today the word describes anything which is manufactured from fibres or yarns (fibres which have been spun together). Cords, ropes, lace and nets are all textiles. Cloth made by weaving, knitting, felting, bonding or tufting is also a textile. Fibres can be either man-made or natural. Cotton and wool are examples of natural fibres. Man-made fibres are made from chemicals and include polyester and nylon.

Textiles for sale in Bahrain

You only have to look around you to see how important textiles are. We use them to make clothes; our houses have curtains, carpets and upholstery all made from textiles. And there are many industrial uses of textiles too. String, tents and parachutes are just a few examples.

Different textiles have different properties. Some are stronger than others, some are warmer. The textile we choose for a particular job depends on the job it is going to do.

The inset shows textile fibres magnified several times

PLANT FIBRES – COTTON

We get some of the fibres used to make textiles from plants. The most widely used plant fibre is cotton – in fact it accounts for half of all the natural fibres used by the world's textile industry. Cotton grows as soft, white fibres attached to the seeds of the cotton plant. The clumps of fibres are called cotton bolls. A typical boll can contain half a million fibres! First, the cotton has to be picked from the plant. This can be done by machine or hand. Once it has been picked, the cotton must be separated from the seeds. This process is called "ginning". The cotton fibres are then pressed together into large bales ready to be transported by road or rail.

Ginning

The harvested cotton is first fed onto a revolving roller beater. Here the leaves and dirt – known as trash – are beaten free from the fibres. The cotton seeds fall into a separate trough for use as cattle food. The fibres are blown by a fan onto the rough surface of a large revolving roller (the gin). A fan also blows the separated fibres from the gin. They are then ready to be spun.

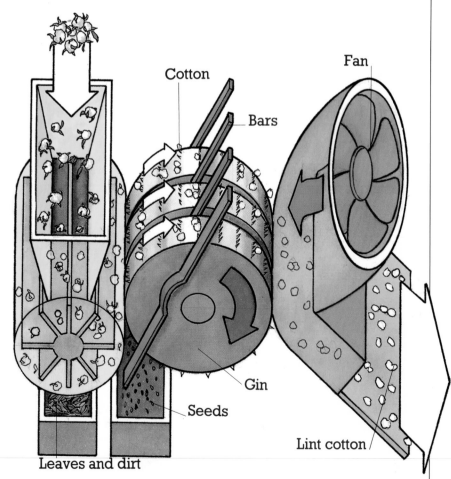

Cotton

Bars

Fan

Gin

Seeds

Lint cotton

Leaves and dirt

7

Cotton being harvested in Australia

ANIMAL FIBRES – WOOL

Most of the wool we use comes from sheep. When the sheep's coat (called the fleece) is removed it is usually very dirty and coated in lanolin – a natural grease produced by the sheep to help keep itself warm. Both the dirt and the lanolin have to be removed by sorting and washing. During a process called scouring, the wool is passed through warm baths containing chemicals which dissolve the dirt. It is then rinsed and dried.

By this time the wool is very tangled. All the fibres face in different directions, so the wool has to be fed through a carding machine. This has rollers covered in tiny wire teeth which comb through the fibres.

Wool has many useful characteristics. It is warm to wear, stretches and can absorb water without feeling wet. Most of our wool comes from sheep but smaller quantities come from the animals in the picture.

Bactrian camel

Alpaca

Merino sheep

Cashmere goat

Angora goat

Karakul sheep

A shearer can shear a sheep in four minutes

SILK

All caterpillars spin cocoons around themselves while they change into moths or butterflies. But some, called silkworms, spin their cocoons from a thread which can be used to make the strong, shiny fabric we call silk. The silkworm also produces a gum which helps to hold the thread together and harden the cocoon.

The silkworms inside the cocoon are killed so the silk can be used. First, the cocoon is dropped in very hot water. This loosens the thread from the gum so it can be unwound. The fine threads (filaments) from three or more cocoons are usually unwound together to form a thread that is strong enough to be woven or knitted.

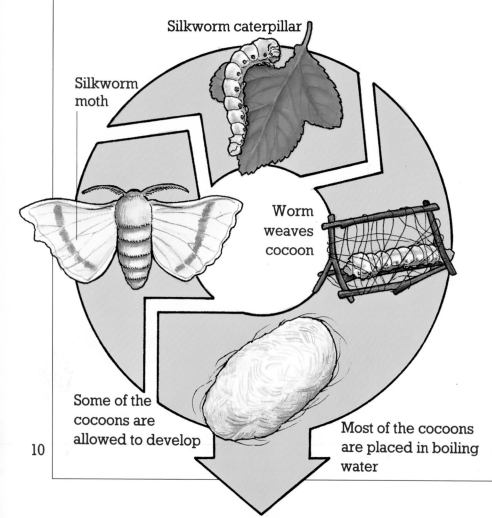

Silkworm caterpillar

Silkworm moth

Worm weaves cocoon

Some of the cocoons are allowed to develop

Most of the cocoons are placed in boiling water

The adult silkworm lays its eggs on mulberry leaves. Silkworm caterpillars hatch from these eggs and start to feed on the leaves. They eat for 30 days and moult four times before they start to spin a cocoon. The silkworm produces silk thread from two tiny holes below its mouth called spinnerets. It spins for two or three days until it is encased. Adult moths emerge from the cocoons but on a silk farm most silkworms are killed in their cocoons for their silk threads.

Chinese silkworms make high quality silk

Unwinding the silk from the silkworms' cocoons

MAN-MADE FIBRES

Natural fibres provide us with textiles which are comfortable to wear. But they have some disadvantages. Cotton creases easily, wool tends to shrink and none of them are hard wearing. Man-made fibres can be used to make clothes which are easier to wash, do not crease or shrink and are also cheaper. However, they are not so comfortable. Man-made fibres may be made from a chemical called cellulose which comes from plants such as wood. Or they may be made from chemicals found in coal and oil. Plastics (which also come from oil) can be used to make fabrics. Fibres of nylon, polyester and acrylic are twisted into yarns for making cloth.

Viscose is made from the cellulose in wood. Water is mixed with wood and a chemical called caustic soda which dissolves the cellulose fibres. These fibres are made into cellulose sheets and mixed with another chemical, carbon disulphide. This mixture is left to soak in a bath of caustic soda for a few days. It forms a syrupy liquid. This is squirted through a spinneret (a nozzle full of tiny holes) into sulphuric acid. It finally forms long thin fibres of viscose.

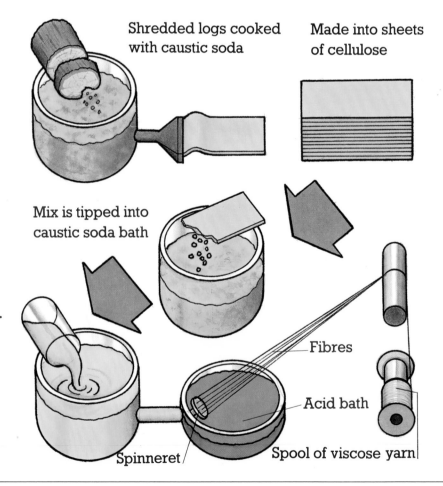

Shredded logs cooked with caustic soda

Made into sheets of cellulose

Mix is tipped into caustic soda bath

Fibres

Acid bath

Spinneret

Spool of viscose yarn

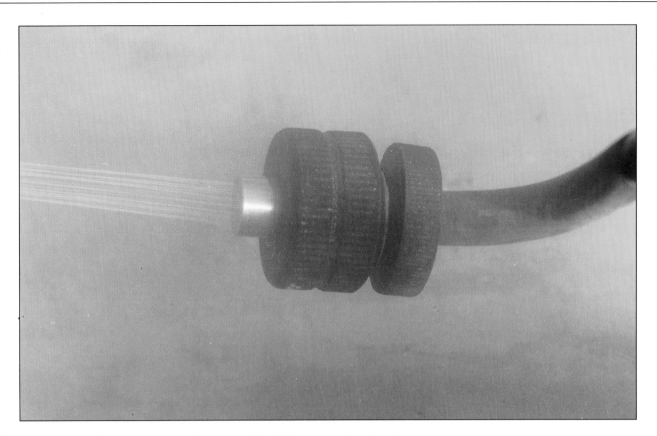

A man-made spinneret showing the filaments hardening

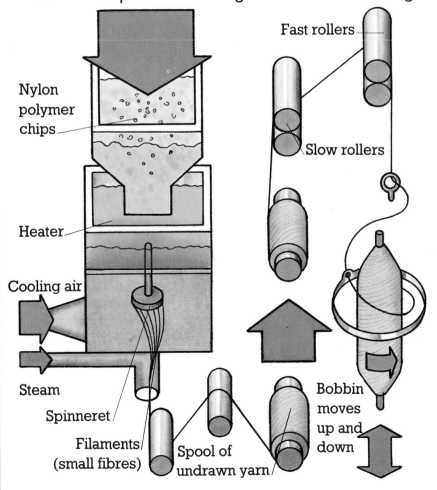

Nylon polymer chips

Heater

Cooling air

Steam

Spinneret

Filaments (small fibres)

Spool of undrawn yarn

Fast rollers

Slow rollers

Bobbin moves up and down

Nylon is made from chemicals which are found in oil. When the chemicals are heated they form a liquid which is made up of very long molecules called polymers. The liquid is forced through a spinneret and cooled so that the polymers harden into a series of endless filaments. These are wound onto a spool and then fed through a series of rollers. The filaments are stretched by these rollers before being wound onto a spinning bobbin. The long filaments can now be chopped up to make short fibres of nylon.

13

SPINNING

Most natural fibres – except for silk – are too short and weak to be used as they are. They have to be spun into stronger, longer yarns before they can be used to make textiles. Often the fibres are still dirty and tangled when they arrive at the spinning mill and have to be to cleaned and combed. These processes may be carried out by machines. The fibres leave them as ropes of clean, straightened fibres which are called slivers. Several slivers are stretched by rollers and twisted together slightly to form a roving. The spinning process, in which the roving is stretched and twisted into a fine thread and wound onto a bobbin, can now begin.

The first rollers squeeze the fibres together into a mat which is then fed onto wire-toothed rollers. These rollers comb out the tangled fibres.

A number of vertical rollers divide the sections called slivers. The slivers are collected in sliver bins where they wait for the next stage.

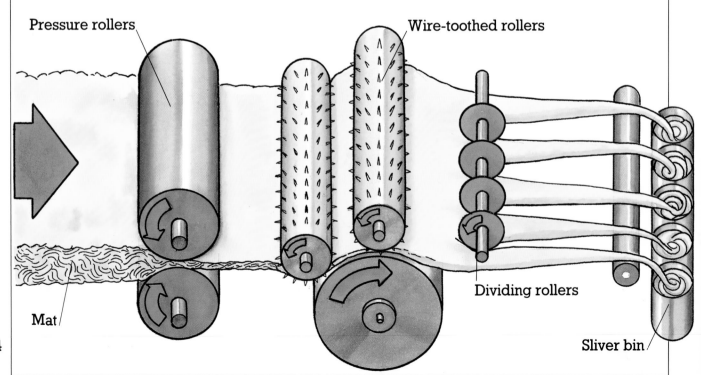

Pressure rollers

Wire-toothed rollers

Mat

Dividing rollers

Sliver bin

Slivers being converted into rovings ready for spinning

Several slivers are fed together between slowly rotating rollers which twist them into a single roving. The roving is wound onto a bobbin.

Yet more rollers stretch the roving and twist it into a finer and finer thread. The spinning process is now complete and the final thread is collected on a bobbin.

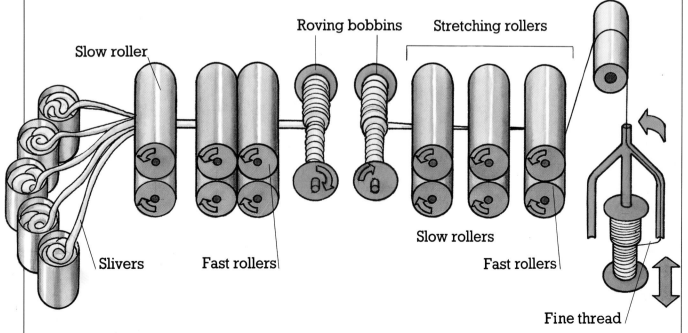

Roving bobbins   Stretching rollers

Slow roller

Slivers   Fast rollers

Slow rollers

Fast rollers

Fine thread

WEAVING

Once the yarns have been prepared they can be woven to make fabrics. A woven fabric is made up of yarns (or threads) which run lengthways (the warp threads) and widthways (the weft threads). In the simplest woven fabric, weft threads pass over and under the warp threads.

Weaving is done on a machine called a loom which is usually fully automated. The warp threads are stretched, parallel to each other, along the length of the loom. The weft thread, which is carried by a shuttle, passes between the warp threads as they are raised or lowered. By raising different warp threads, different patterns can be obtained in the fabric.

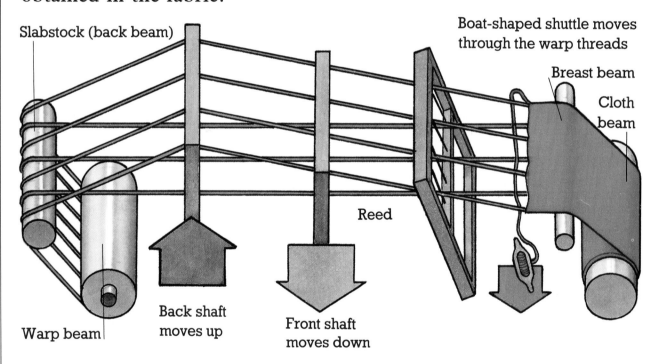

Slabstock (back beam)

Boat-shaped shuttle moves through the warp threads

Breast beam

Cloth beam

Reed

Back shaft moves up

Front shaft moves down

Warp beam

The diagram shows how a simple loom works. The warp threads are unwound from the warp beam and stretch along the length of the loom to the cloth beam at the other end.

Alternate warp threads pass through the back shaft while the rest are threaded through the front shaft. When the back shaft is raised a gap forms between the two lots of warp threads.

Wool is woven into a tartan fabric in Scotland

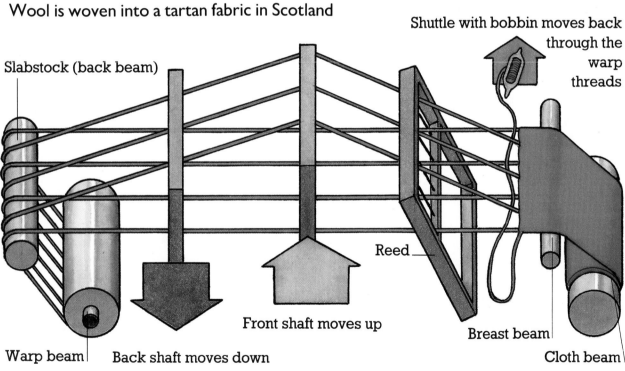

Slabstock (back beam)

Shuttle with bobbin moves back through the warp threads

Reed

Front shaft moves up

Warp beam   Back shaft moves down

Breast beam

Cloth beam

The weft thread is carried by a shuttle. The shuttle passes through the gap in the warp threads. When the shafts change position the shuttle returns again ready to repeat the process.

The reed pushes the weft threads tightly down on the developing cloth. As the process is repeated again and again, the newly-formed cloth is wound onto the cloth beam.

KNITTING AND FELTING

Knitting is another way of turning yarns into fabrics. Knitted fabrics are very different from woven ones – they are looser and stretchier. A knitted fabric is made by forming the yarn into loops or stitches which are linked together.

There are two main ways of knitting. Weft knitting uses just one continuous length of yarn which is used to make loops across the width of the fabric. This sort of knitting can be done by hand on needles or it can be done more quickly by machine. Weft knitting is used to make clothes. Warp knitting is used to make fabrics for cloths and carpets. Felting is another way of making fabric without weaving. Felt is made by pressing together woollen fibres.

Tennis balls are covered with a layer of felt

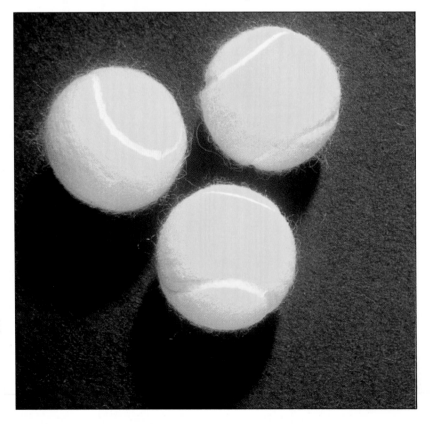

Felt is a compact fabric made from wet woollen fibres. First the wet fibres are tangled together. Then they are heated before being pressed together to allow the fibres to shrink. The tangled fibres form a dense mat cloth which can be easily cut in pieces of different shapes. This cloth can be dyed and is suitable for making hats and covering tennis balls. Billiard tables are usually covered with a thin layer of green felt.

The diagram shows a section of weft knitting. It shows clearly how the weft yarn is loosely looped around itself to form a fabric.

Knitting can be done by super-fast machines

DYEING AND PRINTING

The natural colour of fibres is off-white. To make fabrics more attractive they may be dyed or printed. Dyes are coloured chemicals, either natural or man-made, which stick to the fibres. Almost all fabrics are bleached to make them white first, even if they are to be dyed. This makes them better able to absorb the dyes. The fabric can then be passed through a dye bath. It is important to make sure that the dye sticks evenly through the fabric.

If patterns of different colours are required, different coloured yarns can be used. Or the fabric may be printed. Unlike dyeing, the dyes used during printing do not soak through the fabric but stick to one side only.

Silk screen printing

A different silk screen is made for each colour which is printed. To make the screen, the silk is treated with a chemical which stops ink passing through it. But some areas are not treated and allow the ink through. The first screen is placed on the fabric and green ink is forced through parts of it. The flowers are printed in a similar way using a second screen. By using a number of different screens, colourful and complicated patterns can be printed. Silk screen printing has many uses and can be used to decorate fabric and paper.

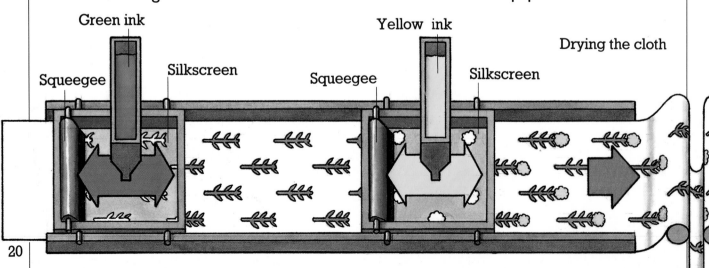

Green ink

Yellow ink

Drying the cloth

Squeegee   Silkscreen

Squeegee   Silkscreen

21

Textiles can be coloured by dipping them in pots of dye .

FINISHING TOUCHES

Cotton textiles do not all have the same characteristics – neither do woollen ones. Cotton and wool can be treated in different ways to produce slightly different textiles. Cotton and linen fabrics have their creases smoothed out and are given a smooth glossy surface finish. Wool fabrics are steamed and pressed to remove creases. Cotton can be treated with caustic soda solution to turn it into seersucker or poplin which is glossy like silk. Woollen fabrics may be brushed to make them suitably soft for making blankets and coats. The diagrams below show some of the ways woollen fabrics are treated to give them their final characteristics.

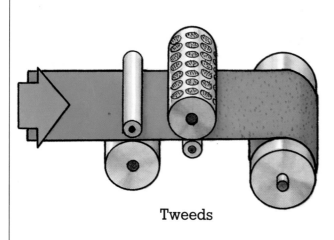

Tweeds

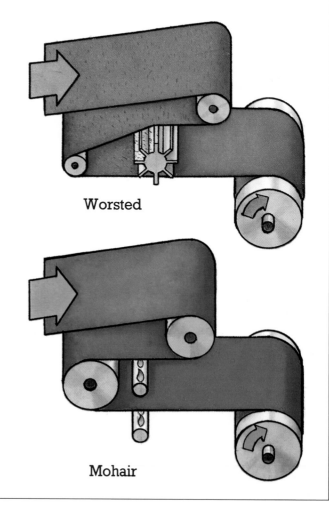

Worsted

Mohair

The surface of tweed and worsted which are both strong and smooth are raised by being pushed through prickly revolving drums. This makes them more comfortable to wear. Mohair has a very "hairy" surface. It is passed over a gas flame which burns off the longest hairs which would otherwise tickle when the fabric was worn.

Extra thick warp

Wefts

Warps

The thick warp threads of a carpet are cut to form the pile. This makes the carpet springy to walk on and warmer to touch.

23

A wool carpet being woven on a loom

SPECIAL TREATMENTS

After fabrics have been coloured there are still other processes they can be put through to improve them in some way. For example, fabrics for tents or raincoats are given a coating of resin to make them waterproof. Wool can be treated with chemicals to protect it from being eaten by moth larvae. A chemical process called chlorination is used to prevent fabrics from shrinking. Other fabrics are simply preshrunk to prevent shrinking when they are washed. Chemicals can be used to put permanent creases in clothes such as pleated skirts. Fireproofing textiles is very important, especially for children's clothes and protective clothing for firemen.

Fabric such as cotton can be made waterproof by treating it with plastic. The fabric is passed around a series of rollers and into a bath containing plastic paste. The plastic soaks into the fabric. As it emerges from the bath it is heated to help the plastic to soak evenly into the fabric. Finally, a cooling process makes the plastic harden and stay in place on the fabric. A similar process is used to impregnate fabrics with a variety of chemicals. Textiles can be fire-proofed by using chemicals that do not burn easily.

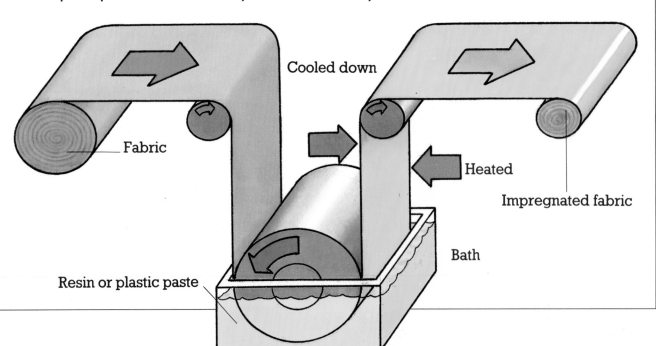

Cooled down

Fabric

Heated

Impregnated fabric

Bath

Resin or plastic paste

A plastic coating makes clothing waterproof

THE STORY OF A PAIR OF JEANS

1. COTTON IS PICKED EITHER BY HAND OR BY MACHINE AND THEN PROCESSED (GINNING).

2. THE RAW COTTON IS SENT TO THE TEXTILE MILL WHERE THE LOOSE, FLUFFY FIBRES ARE FORMED INTO A LONG SHEET AND THEN ROLLED. THIS IS THEN MADE INTO LONG SOFT ROPES BEFORE FINALLY BEING SPUN INTO YARN.

5. THE FIRST STEP IN THE CREATION OF THE JEANS IS THE DESIGNING WHICH INDICATES THE TYPE OF STITCHING, POCKETS, FIT AND STYLE. A SAMPLE IS MADE BEFORE THE PATTERNS ARE DRAWN OUT. FOR EACH PAIR OF JEANS THERE ARE TEN DIFFERENT PATTERN PIECES – AS WELL AS RIVETS, BUTTONS OR ZIP **7.** (AS MANY AS 80 DIFFERENT SETS OF PATTERNS CAN BE MADE FOR VARYING SIZES) **6.** THE PATTERNS ARE CUT OUT OF SEVERAL LAYERS OF FABRIC BY HIGH SPEED CUTTERS.

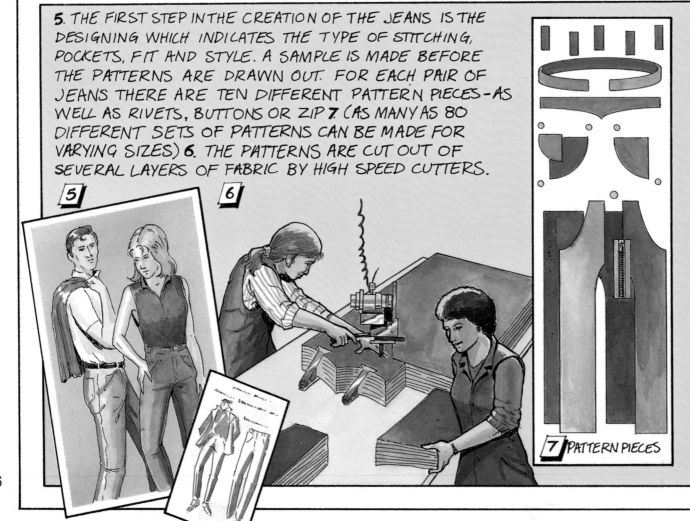

7 PATTERN PIECES

TO MAKE DENIM, THE WARD YARNS ARE DYED A DARK BLUE COLOUR CALLED INDIGO **3**. BEFORE WEAVING **4**. AND THE WEFT YARNS ARE LEFT UNDYED. COTTON DYED WITH INDIGO FADES IN A CERTAIN WAY ON WEARING AND WASHING, WHICH GIVES THE JEANS THEIR CHARACTERISTIC LOOK.

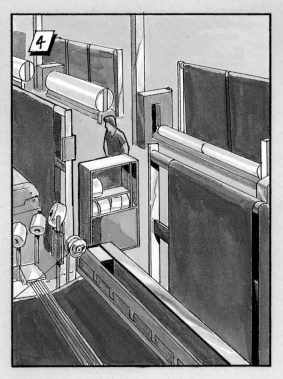

8 SEWING OPERATIONS

1. ASSEMBLING POCKETS, BELT LOOPS AND BACK POCKETS.
2. ATTACHING POCKETS
3. SEWING LEG SEAMS
4. SEWING ON WAISTBAND
5. ATTACHING BELT LOOPS
6. ATTACHING BUTTONS
7. SEWING ON ZIPPER
8. SEWING BOTTOM HEM
9. ATTACHING RIVETS
10. ATTACHING LABEL OF JEAN MAKER.

8. THE DIFFERENT PIECES ARE SEWN TOGETHER BY MACHINES DESIGNED TO DO ONE TYPE OF JOB (THERE ARE TEN DIFFERENT JOBS)
9. FINALLY THE JEANS ARE CHECKED, PRESSED, SIZE TAGS ATTACHED AND SENT TO THE WAREHOUSE WHERE RETAILERS' ORDERS ARE MADE UP AND DISPATCHED.

FACT FILE 1

This map of the world shows where some of the most common natural fibres are produced. You will see that different fibres are produced in different parts of the world. The climate of a country has a lot to do with the fibres it produces. For example, sheep do not breed well in very cold climates so you do not find wool being produced in northern Europe or Canada. Cotton grows well in areas where there is a warm, wet growing season and a dry, warm picking season, such as in parts of the United States. The demand for a particular fibre also affects where it is produced – as does the price it can be sold at. China used to produce a lot of silk. But since the 1930s, when rayon and then nylon became available, the market for silk has dwindled. Both the USA and India grow cotton. But the USA can afford to use more machinery, fertilisers and pesticides. So the USA can produce about fives times as much cotton as India can from the same area of land. The only textile produced in any quantity in the UK is wool. The climate is too cold for plant fibres to grow well.

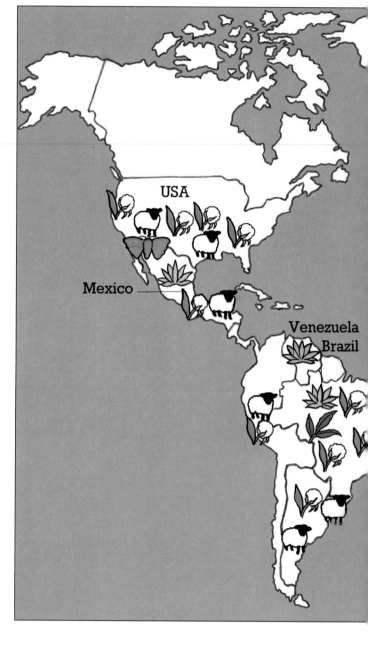

Wool
Most wool is produced in Australia, New Zealand as well as in Africa and South America. Sheep are not found in cold climates.

Cotton
The main cotton producers are the USA, USSR and China. They produce over half the world's cotton.

Silk
Japan produces over two thirds of the world's silk. The other major silk producers are China, the USSR and India.

28

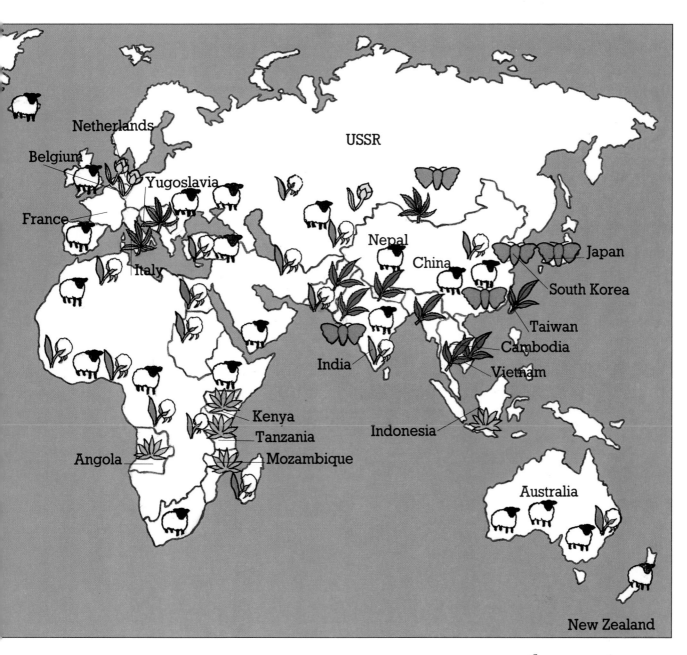

Sisal
Kenya and Tanzania between them grow over half the world's sisal. South America also produces some sisal.

Flax
The USSR grows about two thirds of the world's flax crop. Flax is also grown in Belgium, France and the Netherlands.

Jute/Hemp
Most jute grows in India and Pakistan. The major producers of hemp are the USSR followed by Italy and Yugoslavia.

29

FACT FILE 2

There is huge variety of textiles to choose from. On these pages you will find out where they come from, how they are produced and what they are used for – everything from clothes to life belts.

The largest amount of textiles made by the textile industry goes into the making of clothes. What types of fibres are you wearing? Are they natural or man-made, printed or dyed? As fashions change different textiles become popular. Denim jeans made from cotton are just one example of a successful fashion design which uses cotton. Jute, kapok and hessian are more often used in household furnishings. Carpets are often backed with jute or hessian and cushions are stuffed with kapok.

⬤ Animal   ⬤ Mineral   ⬤ Vegetable

Product	Where it comes from	Method of manufacture	Use
WOOL	Wool comes from sheep, goats, camels, llamas all over the world.	The wool is sheared off, then combed and drawn out. Then it is spun or twisted.	Carpets, clothes, felt and upholstery.
SILK 	Silk nurseries in Japan, China, India, Bulgaria, France, Mexico and Turkey.	The silk threads of the silkworm cocoons are used.	Stockings, dresses and underwear.
FLAX	Flax is grown in damp, cool climates in USSR, Belgium, France and the Netherlands.	The stalks of the plant go through several processes to produce useable fibres.	Linen is used for tablecloths, towels and bedclothes.
COTTON	Cotton is grown in the warm and moist regions of the world.	Cotton goes through several processes until the fibre can be spun.	It is used to make all kinds of clothes.
HEMP	Hemp grows in warm regions of Asia, Europe and North America.	Same as flax.	Rope, twine, canvas and sail cloth.
JUTE	Jute comes from tropical regions such as India and Pakistan.	Same as flax.	It is mainly used as sacking and hessian.

Product	Where it comes from	Method of manufacture	Use
ROMIE (grasscloth)	This is found in the warmer parts of China and Japan.	Same as flax.	Romie is used in the same way as linen.
SISAL	Grows in Eastern Africa, Java and tropical America.	The leaves are cultivated to produce the fibres.	Sisal is used to make ropes, twine, sacking and mats.
KAPOK	Grown in Java, Indonesia and southern parts of Asia.	The tree seed is processed to produce the white fluffy kapok.	Often used as stuffing in upholstery and cushions.
VISCOSE	The main source is from spruce trees.	Viscose is processed from cellulose and wood pulp.	Viscose is used to make clothes.
LUREX	Lurex is made from aluminium mined mainly in South Africa.	The aluminium is coated with fabric.	It is used to make clothes.
ASBESTOS	It is mined in South Africa, Java, tropical America, Canada and Italy.	It is taken from veins in various types of rocks.	Used to fireproof cloth but is known to be a hazard.
POLYAMIDES (Nylon)	These are made from fossil fuels such as oil.	Polymerized – a chemical process that makes plastics – by heating.	Most often used to make clothes and carpets.
POLYESTERS (Terylene)	Made from fossil fuels.	Same as above.	Used for making clothes and carpets.
ACRYLICS (Acrilan)	Made from fossil fuels.	Formed by dissolving chemicals.	Used for making clothes.
MODACRYLICS	Made from fossil fuels.	As above.	Clothes.

GLOSSARY

Bobbin
A reel on which thread is wound.

Fabric
Any cloth made from yarn by weaving, knitting or felting.

Felting
Making a fabric by pressing fibres together.

Fibre
Any hair or fine thread used for spinning into yarn.

Knitting
Making a fabric from one piece of yarn.

Shuttle
A box or stick which carries weft threads through the gap in the warp threads on a loom.

Spinning
Any method of twisting fibres into yarn or the process of forcing liquid through a small hole to make synthetic yarns.

Thread
A fine strand or fibre.

Worsted
A fine, strong, tightly twisted yarn spun from combed wool – or the cloth made from this yarn.

INDEX

32

PRINTED IN BELGIUM BY
proost
INTERNATIONAL BOOK PRODUCTION